MW00900432

Thank you to Kyle, Brandon, my mom, The Front Bottoms and my tumblr followers lmao

I heard you got a new girlfriend

I asked you to tell me about her and you asked me what I wanted
to know and that's when I knew you didn't really love her.
Because if you loved her then you would've told me about how her
eyes light up when she laughs and she bites her lip when she's sad.
You would've told me about the way her teeth remind you of those
glow-in-the-dark stars you stuck on your ceiling when you were
little and the way her voice wraps around your bones and keeps
you from shaking. You would've told me about the tips of her
fingers and the way sunshine pours from her mouth. You would've
told me about how she even looks pretty when she cries and the
way she hides behind her hair. You would've told me about the
way you want to live inside her ribcage and fall asleep in the crook
of her neck. You would've told me that she tastes like the entire
galaxy and she speaks in poetry. You would've told me that the
sound of her breath while she sleeps is your new favorite song.
You would've told me about how she's in your blood and the way
she's got so much love in her veins that if you cut her open, you
swear flowers would grow from inside of her. You would've told
me about the way you love her, like I love you.

For future reference

1. When a boy who leaves goose bumps on every inch of your skin tries to play you his favorite song, don't let him. He'll get it stuck in your head and under your fingertips and when he leaves, you won't be able to listen to it without feeling like you're choking.

2. Don't let him touch you all over no matter how much you want to feel him against you. Leave a few spots untouched so that when you're sleeping alone again, at least your left wrist and an inch of your right hip won't sting with the remaining burn of his mouth.

3. Don't watch the sunset with him. He'll poison it. You won't be able to look at the sky without swallowing a mouthful of him.

4. Don't mistake wasps for butterflies. Sometimes when you feel your stomach flutter and your hands start to shake it's pain, not love.

5. Just because he tells you he loves you doesn't mean he's going to stay.

6. It's okay to delete his number after he kisses the pretty girl he met when he was drunk. It's okay to leave when he hurts you. You don't have to keep falling into him.

7. When he tells you that you're beautiful, try to remember that you were beautiful before him too.

For future reference

8. Just because he reads and smokes cigarettes and talks about the stars doesn't mean he's your soul mate.

9. After you kiss him, remember to wash your mouth out right away so he doesn't burn into your tongue.

10. He'll kiss you in the rain and take you to little coffee shops. He'll brush your hair out of your eyes and kiss your nose. He'll grab your waist and whisper in your ear but six months later you'll find yourself drunk texting him that you miss him and he won't respond.

11. Your heart is going to break a million times. It's going to feel like the world is falling apart around you. Your lungs will stop working some nights. You find yourself grabbing at your bones trying to hold yourself together. You're going to feel like you're dying. It's going to be okay. You'll find someone else to kiss you goodnight.

It's not that I don't love you

It's not that I don't love you. It's the sound I heard when I was 9
and my father slammed the front door so hard behind him I swear
to god it shook the whole house. For the next 3 years I watched my
mother break her teeth on vodka bottles. I think she stopped
breathing when he left. I think part of her died. I think he took her
heart with him when he walked out. Her chest is empty, just a
shattered mess of cracked ribs and depression pills.

It's not that I don't love you. It's all the blood in the sink. It's the
night that I spent 12 hours in the emergency room waiting to see if
my sister was going to be okay, after the boy she loved, told her he
didn't love her anymore. It's the crying, and the fluorescent lights,
and white sneakers and pale faces and shaky breaths and blood. So
much blood.

It's not that I don't love you. It's the time that I had to stay up for
two days straight with my best friend while she cried and shrieked
and threw up on my bedroom floor because her boyfriend fucked
his ex. I swear to god she still has tear streaks stained onto her
cheeks. I think when you love someone, it never really goes away.

It's not that I don't love you. It's the six weeks we had a substitute
in English because our teacher was getting divorced and couldn't
handle getting out of bed. When she came back she was smiling.
But her hands shook so hard when she held her coffee, you could
see that something was broken inside. And sometimes when things

It's not that I don't love you

break, you can't fix them. Nothing ever goes back to how it was. I got an A in English that year. I think her head was always spinning too hard to read any essays.

It's not that I don't love you. It's that I do.

13 voicemails you left me

May 16th// 11:08 pm
"Hey, I guess you're asleep. Call me back when you wake up."

July 24th// 5:04 am
"Wake up I miss you."

September 8th// 2:09 am
"I just wanted to hear your voice."

September 8th// 2:16 am
"Okay listen, I think I might be in love with you please call me back."

October 11th// 5:42 pm
"Baby girl I love you, I'm so happy you're mine I'll see you tonight."

November 29th// 8:06 am
"You're still asleep and you're the most beautiful thing in the world. I can't wait to get home and see you. I can't wait to kiss you."

December 12th// 9:16 am
"Look I'm sorry about what I said. I didn't mean it. I still love you princess. I love you. I'm sorry. I just... I love you alright. Call me back when you can."

13 voicemails you left me

January 15th// 4:06 pm

"I'm out and I saw something that made me think of you so I thought I would call you. I miss your voice."

January 18th// 9:12 am

"Baby get dressed, I'm picking you up in 15, let's run away."

January 23rd// 8:47 pm

"Oh god your mother hates me."

February 14th// 3:06 pm

"Happy Valentine's Day I love you more than anything. You're the world. You're everything good. I'd let you swallow me whole. I like the way you look when you're tired. I hate it when you cry. I'll see you tonight baby."

February 24th// 12:09 am

"I'm sorry."

April 8th// 4:06 am

"Hey… I need to come over and get the rest of my stuff."

But jesus fuck I'd swallow poison if it tasted like you.

I won't say I miss you but I think my mother knows anyway

Listen,
if you're going to leave, that's fine.
and I know you promised you wouldn't
seven months ago while I was crying
into your neck but I also know that
sometimes it rains even when it's not
supposed to and sometimes boys
kiss girls they shouldn't and we tear
flowers out of the ground just to watch
them die and things change,
so I understand if you're done,
but please, when you're packing all your
old sweaters and books, don't forget
to take all your three AM phone calls,
and photographs where we're smiling
so wide it looks like we've never known
that feeling in the pit of your stomach
when someone screams "I don't love you
anymore."
Take back every kiss, every night you
fell asleep next to me, every poem I
wrote you, every song you sang to
me, every "I love you more" fight,
every shock I felt in my skin when
you brushed against me.
I was never scared of ghosts until you

I won't say I miss you but I think my mother knows anyway

left but now I see you everywhere and
god if you're going to kill me please
just do it quickly because I see you
in everything and it's making it hard
to breathe.

9 things to remember when you're 14

1. high school will drain you. it's panic attacks in the hallway and crying in the bathroom and eating lunch in the back of the library because the cafeteria makes your heart beat too fast. It's getting high and throwing up. you will learn a lot about death and how to treat your cuts. You will also learn what it's like to get drunk and laugh at the stars and how to write poetry that makes the world hurt less. You will read books that you fall in love with. you will fall in love. you'll get closer to your mother because you'll need someone to help you with your math homework and teach you how to put on your makeup and wipe away your tears.

2. the first boy you fall in love with will break you. he'll tell you he loves you and convince you to fuck him in the back of his parents' beat up Volvo and then he'll tell all his friends what you taste like and stop calling you before you fall asleep. delete his number and throw away the stuffed bear he won you at the carnival three weeks before. your carpet will be stained with tears and vomit and liquor and you'll fight with your dad a lot more than usual. you'll spit up pieces of your heart for weeks. you'll burn alive when you see him in the halls. you won't always feel like you're cracking and a few months later you'll be falling asleep on the phone with someone else. let it hurt for a little while but don't let it kill you. never let it kill you.

9 things to remember when you're 14

3. the girl you've been best friends with for 9 years will stop speaking to you. one night you'll make plans with her and she'll cancel at the last minute because she's sick but you'll see her updating her snapchat story with pictures of empty alcohol bottles and blurry eyes and the mean girls who never let you sit with them. try to forgive her. she's going through all the bloody, broken teeth, black and blue filled nights like you are. everyone's trying to survive so don't be too hard on anyone. especially yourself.

4. your teacher will ask the class questions and you'll know the answers but you'll keep your shaky hand between your knees and keep your tongue glued to the top of your mouth. don't bother. speak out. nothing bad will happen. so when your biology teachers calls on you to tell him about last night's assignment, don't stare at the spinning ground and mumble through numb lips. you're smarter than you think and nobody is looking at you anyway.

5. you're not his baby girl. when he tries to kiss your neck and pull you onto his lap, get up and leave. you don't have to go upstairs with him. you don't have to sleep with him because he's begging. it's not your job to fuck around with boys who can't remember your name. take care of yourself even when he's calling you a tease and whispering just loud enough for you to hear.

9 things to remember when you're 14

6. go out. go to football games and sit on hard metal bleachers for hours and take shots that taste like bleach and hold hands with the cute boy from English class. go to that dumb party and don't complain or stand in the corner. things are always moving. people are always falling in love and laughing and putting themselves back together. be part of it.

7. ask for help. you don't have to let yourself rot. when you don't know how to do something in math class ask your teacher to explain. when your heart falls out of your chest and shatters at your feet, ask your best friend to come over and watch bad movies with you until you both feel less dead. when the boy you're convinced you love kisses someone else, ask your mother to help stop the bleeding. you're not alone so stop acting like it. no more breakdowns at three in the morning locked in the bathroom screaming. your older sister is still awake. crawl into bed with her.

8. it all ends. high school doesn't last forever and 6 years from now you'll be whole again. you won't remember the names of the boys who made you cry or the girls who fucked you over. you won't remember the names of the teachers who made your cheeks turn red and tied your stomach in knots. you won't remember the time you fell down the stairs in front of everyone. you won't remember what it's like to want to die. try to remember the times you laughed so hard you spit out your drink. try to remember the people who helped put you back together. try to remember the people who bled

9 things to remember when you're 14

with you when things got messy. when they call you at 3 in the
morning to ask how you've been, answer the phone.

9. don't forget to breathe.

my mother's trust issues are leaking into my chest

and I've got my father's nose and his tendency to

stop calling back

so I'm sorry

about the 9 missed calls I have from you

and the 6 voicemails I never played

I swear I'd love you if I could

And I think the thing that terrifies me most is that one day, you'll be the story I'll tell my daughter, when she's curled up in bed, wrapped in blankets and heartbreak, when she hasn't eaten anything in days but the voicemails he left her, when she hasn't been able to sleep because the goodbye that broke her shatters her bones all over again every time she closes her fucking eyes. And I'll climb into bed with her and she'll lay her head on my lap and I'll try to brush him out of her hair and her tears will soak through my shirt and I'll tell her about the boy I met when I was sixteen, who sat next to me in math class, who I fell in love with after two weeks, who saved me, who fucking destroyed me. And I'll tell her about how it hurt. It hurt so badly it almost killed me. It hurt so badly my mother stopped going to work so she could stay home and make sure I didn't take too many pills. And then I'll tell her about how it got better. How it stopped hurting. How I stopped bleeding. My mother went back to work. I got out of bed. But I won't tell her that sometimes I still have dreams about you and can hardly breathe the next day or about the pictures of you I have hidden in the attic.

How it happens

I think when you're 16 you don't expect it to hurt as much as it
does
but what the fuck would you know about love till it slams into your
chest and knocks the wind out of your lungs
so you fall in love
and he leaves
and you stop washing your hair
and your skin is bruised with the creases in your sheets
and your mother wants to yell at you but your blank stare just
makes her eyes tear up and you're not supposed to see your mother
cry
and you'll probably try destroying yourself because that's what
you do when you're 16
so you'll pull apart razors and hide them someplace your parents
can find them but they never do
and you'll start smoking even though it makes you cough so hard
you throw up and you can't stand the burning in your throat
and you'll run away without ever leaving your bedroom
and maybe you'll kiss too many boys who mean nothing but mean
all too much and they will all look a little like him or nothing at all
and you let him fuck you up
and you leave him drunk voicemails and you haven't cried in 23
days even though you're always crying
and you promise you will never love anything again because it
hurts more than they warned
no one told you that this was love

How it happens

and maybe it's not love
maybe it's more
maybe it's something from another world
maybe it's just your bones breaking again
either way it fucking burns
and now you're older
and you know to expect to come out the other side missing a few
pieces of yourself
but sometimes you get caught up and you forgot that it's supposed
to hurt
because it's not supposed to fucking hurt
and you blink and you're bleeding again
and it's like you're 16 all over again
trying to rip yourself to shreds while you try to pick up all the
pieces of yourself
everyone thinks you're mysterious because your mouth is sewn
shut with the sudden death of past loves but you're just so fucking
quiet because they've taken so much out of you, you can hardly
open your eyes, forget about your mouth,
and I guess the worst part about love dying out is that you don't die
with it,
you just attend the funeral and visit the grave every time you're
drunk. you're always so goddamn drunk.

Heartbreak is not always blood and crushed ribs and waking up in the middle of the night because you were choking on your own tears in your sleep.

Sometimes it's simply standing in the middle of the supermarket, trying not to throw up on the floor and attempting to stop your teeth from chattering and figuring out which loaf of bread you're getting a better deal on at the same time.

Something my mom said over breakfast

What defines a relationship is the way you fight
because when things are good, they're good.
Pay attention to the way things are when they're bad
and the way he treats you when he's mad at you
or the way he reacts when you're angry with him
and whether it's "I love you, you idiot" or a door slammed on your
fingers.

Things work out for us in every universe but this one

1. In one universe only the two of us can breathe underwater and the bottom of the ocean is where we first said "I love you."

2. In another, time resets and we fall for each other all over again every time.

3. We are flowers growing alone on opposite sides of the field but a little girl and her mother pluck us from our homes and put us in a vase where we wilt together.

4. Here, the sky changes color and you can touch each other through the wind so every time I feel a breeze on the back of my neck I know it's your mouth and I smile, you feel the wind whistle through your teeth.

5. This universe we were the same age. We learned to drive at the same time and spent hours driving to see each other even just for one night and never minded radio station static or the way your back always starts to ache in the car.

6. We grew up together, you lived down the street, running down hills together and holding hands when it snowed. You were there when I turned six. You were there when I turned sixteen. You loved me the whole time.

7. You never kissed that girl, I wasn't scared of heights. Your

Things work out for us in every universe but this one

parents didn't fight, I wasn't so far away. We both got enough sleep.

8. We never screamed "I hate you" at each other that one night when we fought over dinner at your older sister's house. We never forgot that we loved each other.

9. We could live in outer space. We bought our own star and always took pictures of each other to hang on the walls. You never got tired of me. We could breathe there in a way we never could here.

10. You only lived an hour away instead of the other side of the world. I never cried. Neither of us knew what tears tasted like.

sometimes,

someone doesn't love you the way they did last winter

and "I don't feel okay"

goes from coming to your house even though they're scared of

driving on the highway at night

to "I'm sorry, feel better"

and they don't take pictures of you anymore

or watch you when you aren't looking

and they still kiss you

but never your forehead or nose

Love me like I love you

I want that undeniable kind of love

when your mom asks about me
I hope your cheeks turn pink and you have to keep your lips
pressed shut because if you open your mouth you won't be able to
keep from telling her how fucking in love you are

the kind of love you wear on all of your clothes
even on your skin
and between strands of hair

the kind of love everyone can see, even when the two of us are on
opposite sides of the room

the kind of love that you can see in pictures
and hear in my voice
I want my voice to sound like love
I want strangers to speak to me and think
"wow, she's in love."

I hope you never bite me out of the tips of your fingernails
or rinse me out of your hair

I hope you never shrug me off or tell your dad that we're only
friends

because I've had that kind of love

Love me like I love you

love that you can brush under the carpet when you need to
the kind of love that disappears while you kiss her but comes back
the second you see me

I don't want the kind of love that you can ignore,

I want that in your fucking face, in your mouth, in your hair, in
your teeth, on your sleeves kind of love.

I bite my lip when I miss you
and lately my mouth has been so
full of blood I can barely speak
I'm not even sure if it's my own
blood. My mother is worried Jesus
Christ, I'm worried. You say you
lost feelings but I lost my fucking mind.

Fuck. It's ironic how empty I am because I swear 6 months ago I had the universe inside of me but I cried the rivers in my bones dry. The volcanoes in my chest erupted when you told me you didn't love me anymore and lava flooded my body and hardened till I stopped sleeping. I had stars in my lungs but I burned them all out with the cigarettes I was smoking to get you the fuck out of my throat. The flowers growing at the bottom of my stomach are dead. Apparently you can't water flowers with vodka. I had the sky in my veins but it's been pretty fucking stormy since I ripped them open. I had planets on the tip of my tongue but the debris from the shattered remains of "us" have been crashing into them. I was everything, And then I met you and we were everything. Now you're fucking some blonde girl who gets high all the time and I'm a fucking mess.

I'm always tired but never of u

Posted: 9 months ago on Jun 30,2015 at 11:25 PM
Notes: 171658
Tags: #anyway

They say you always hurt the ones you love the most.

You must've loved me more than anything.

You touched my thigh and told me you'd be good for me

but you've been turning hearts into tombstones since you learned how to kiss.

You don't know what good is

but you're the best fucking thing I've ever touched

and I'm starting to wish I had listened to my mother

when she said

boys that taste like god will fuck you up.

CPSIA information can be obtained
at www.ICGtesting.com
Printed in the USA
BVHW081935310322
632889BV00006B/1879

9 781365 035425